Berry Pomeroy Castle

DEVON

STEWART BROWN

As one descends into a wooded and secluded Devon valley, the romantic ruin of Berry Pomeroy Castle emerges somewhat unexpectedly through the dense tree canopy. The castle was built in the fifteenth century as a fortified house belonging to the Pomeroy family, and is set within an ancient deer park which would have provided good hunting.

In 1547 the castle was bought by Edward Seymour, Protector of the Realm, uncle and governor of the boy-king Edward VI. Edward Seymour's descendants built a fine country house within the old defences, and about 1600 started an ambitious plan of enlargement which was never completed. The castle was abandoned sometime between 1688 and 1701, when the family moved their main home to Wiltshire. It was left to fall into decay, and quickly became overgrown and steeped in mystery, folklore and legends. This illustrated handbook provides a guide to the castle, its architecture and archaeology, followed by a short history.

Contents

Published by English Heritage,
23 Savile Raw, London Wl S 2ET
Copyright © English Heritage 1997
First published by English Heritage 1997, reprinted 2003, 2006

Photograph by English Heritage Photographic Unit
and copyright of English Heritage, unless otherwise stated.

Printed by the colourhouse
SL C40 03/06 04883
ISBN 1-85074-671-0

Introduction

Watercolour of Berry Pomeroy by Frank Gardiner, 1986

Berry Pomeroy Castle was built in the late fifteenth century as the main family seat of the Pomeroys, an ancient, baronial family who first came to Devon at the time of the Norman Conquest. One of the main attractions of the site was the good hunting offered by the surrounding deer park, which had existed from at least the thirteenth century. Hunting was an important social pastime for the nobility in the medieval period; so was the feasting that followed.

Like most late-medieval castles built by ancient landed families and manorial lords, its defences were mainly intended to protect the immediate household and possessions, and to ward off small-scale attacks by brigands and troublesome neighbours. It is doubtful whether the castle could have withstood a major assault. Such displays of defence provided the owners with symbols of power and status. The building of the castle therefore fulfilled most, if not all, of the Pomeroys' needs: security, social standing and pleasurable pursuits. The inclusion of a chapel provided for their spiritual welfare.

The Pomeroys chose to build on a rocky promontory overlooking a deep ravine carved through limestone by the Gatcombe Brook. The castle was protected by steep natural slopes on three sides, but was vulnerable to attack from the south, where the ground is at first flat, then rises on to a high ridge with commanding views of the castle buildings. On this side, the Pomeroys dug into the rock to form a defensive ditch, or dry moat, which must have had a bridge leading across it to the gatehouse. The ditch has since been infilled, but traces of it survive towards the east.

The precise date when the castle was constructed is not recorded. The first written reference appears in a document dating from 1496, when a third of the castle was assigned to the widow of Richard Pomeroy: 'For her third of the honour and castle of Bury, a great chamber beyond the castle gate with cellar on the left of the gate, with two chambers beyond and belonging to the said great chamber, a kitchen, a larderhouse and a chamber beyond the kitchen.' The lack of references to the castle among the earlier family records suggests that it had not been standing long. The ample provision of gun ports (eleven survive), some showing advanced military design for the period, also suggests a date in the later fifteenth century, quite possibly contemporary in date with the construction of the nearby artillery forts at Dartmouth (1480s and 1490s) and Kingswear (probably 1501-2).

Recent archaeological work indicates little or no occupation before this date, so it is doubtful whether there was an earlier castle, although the site is a fitting one for a small Norman fortification. It is possible that the castle could have supplanted a small building such as a hunting lodge which would have left little trace. Written records show that the Pomeroys occupied a manor house in their manor of Berry Pomeroy from at least the thirteenth century, but this stood on a different site in the nearby village of Berry Pomeroy, next to the church.

In 1547 the castle was bought by Edward Seymour, first Duke of Somerset, uncle and governor of Edward VI, and Protector of England. Protector Somerset, as he was known, was executed in 1552 by political rivals. His eldest son, Sir Edward Seymour, found himself in difficult circumstances, both at court and also with regard to his inheritance. He decided to start a new life in Devon and settled at Berry Pomeroy. In about 1560 he began to replace the Pomeroy domestic buildings with a new house built in a more fashionable style for the period. This was a tall, compact country house with three wings or ranges around an inner courtyard.

West façade of the Seymour house

An artist's impression of the castle, showing it as it might have looked had the north terrace been built. (From a reconstruction by H Gordon Slade, drawn by Terry Ball)

The house was built entirely within the old castle defences, which were left standing, and occupied the eastern half of the site. The remains of this Elizabethan house survive four storeys high to roof level.

Edward managed his property well, and built up a considerable estate which he passed to his eldest son when he died in 1593. This son, also called Edward, soon embarked on an ambitious building programme which was intended to greatly enlarge and improve the house. A magnificent new wing containing state rooms was built along the north-west side of the site, extending beyond the limits of the old defences. This new range looked out across the Gatcombe Valley instead of inwards, and contained a parlour, a great chamber and a great hall with a fashionable, classical-style loggia (covered walkway) placed in front of its main entrance. At the west end was a tall kitchen with spacious lodgings above. The top floor was occupied by a splendid long gallery which stretched for 207ft (63m).

Terraces were begun at both ends of this range and another was planned on its north-west side, overlooking an attractive series of fish ponds in the valley below, but these terraces were abandoned before completion. Another range of rooms, probably intended for services, was planned to extend over the infilled moat along the west side of the site, but this was never started.

The site was abandoned some time between 1688 and 1701, and the buildings were shortly afterwards stripped of valuable building materials. The remains became clad in ivy and soon became the subject of ghostly stories. By the end of the eighteenth century, the site enjoyed the reputation of a picturesque ruin, and it has been much visited over the past three centuries.

Description and Tour

The late fifteenth-century gatehouse and curtain wall, with the Seymour house beyond

The Pomeroy Defences

Gatehouse

The gatehouse (**1**) protected the entrance to the castle and was strongly defended. Originally there was a dry moat (deep ditch) crossed by a bridge in front of the castle, but the moat has since been infilled. The gateway was defended by six gun ports (an opening, or one of a series of openings in a wall for firing guns through) looking out from the ground-floor rooms of the two flanking towers, and from overhead by a slot (machicolation) through which stones and sharp projectiles could be thrown down on attackers.

Just inside the gate arch is a vertical groove which once held a portcullis. This was a gate which could be dropped into position at a moment's notice, and later raised by winding gear in the guardrooms above. Half-way through the gate passage, the arch vault becomes higher and changes to a flatter shape. The inner arch was added when the builders changed their plans for the gatehouse to include a large first-floor hall above.

Pass through into the courtyard and turn right, then right again, up the steps to the first floor of the gatehouse. The gatehouse chamber or hall was re-roofed in 1983. Its most striking feature is a granite arcade dividing off an 'aisle' which opens into two bays, one at each end, formed by the projecting towers. The easternmost bay was screened off (the present wooden screen is a modern replacement) and once contained an altar. On the east wall of this bay is a fine wall-painting showing the Three Kings bearing gifts to the infant Christ. It dates from about the year 1500. The whole gatehouse chamber might have served as the castle chapel, with the screened enclosure as its sanctuary. Equally, the enclosure may have served as a small gatehouse oratory, with the main family chapel situated elsewhere on the site. A fireplace in the chamber would have kept occupants warm in winter. On the left side of the fireplace is an oven (now largely blocked by later masonry) which may have been used to bake bread for religious services.

Above each of the bays you can see the remains of second-floor guardrooms, the wooden floors of which have long since rotted away and disappeared. These also

Wall painting in the gatehouse chamber showing the Adoration of the Three Kings

The gatehouse chamber, which may once have served as the family chapel

served as windlass rooms where the guards turned winding gear to raise and lower the portcullis. The windlass (winding drum) extended between these two rooms and lifted the gate with ropes, chains and pulleys. Counterbalancing weights were probably used to make the task easier. The guardrooms originally had strong slate slab roofs, supported and reinforced by three layers of stout timbers set in sockets in the walls and on projecting corbel stones.

Stone stairs lead down from either end of the hall to the tower basements. From the west end, a wall passage leads to a spiral staircase which rises to the wall-top battlements. Sentries used the passage and stairs to patrol the defences. At the end of the passage is a latrine.

Rampart and curtain wall

Leaving the gatehouse, you follow the remains of the curtain wall which once encircled and protected the fifteenth-century castle. The curtain wall has arrow slits which could have been used for cross bows. At a higher level are the remains of a wall walk for sentries. The wall walk projects a little over the inner face of the wall on corbelled slates. The curtain wall was constructed to face an earthwork rampart which was built up in layers of clay and rubble (**2**). The rampart was built first to give the defences their shape, and was completed before any of the fifteenth-century masonry was erected. A little over half-way along the length of the curtain wall is a projecting door jamb - this is all that remains above ground of the original domestic buildings inside the Pomeroy castle. At the far end of the rampart walk, on the right, is St Margaret's tower.

St Margaret's tower

St Margaret's tower (**3**) is U-shaped and projects from the south-east corner of the castle into the moat to give gunners good sighting and firing lines along the defences. The basement of the tower has a cupboard, probably for keeping gunpowder dry, a lamp bracket, and the remains of three gun ports with triple openings for firing three

View of the rampart terrace and wall walk

first floor is a later insertion, probably dating from the mid-sixteenth century.

The Seymour House
South range: kitchen and service rooms

Leaving the fifteenth-century buildings, you now enter the Elizabethan house erected by the Seymours a little over fifty years later. The Seymour house was a tall, compact house built around an open inner courtyard, and comprising three ranges or wings (south, west and north). There are a number of differences between the Pomeroy and Seymour buildings. The building stone chosen by the Pomeroys is a dark green-grey slate from a nearby quarry (the present car park), whereas the

The exterior of St Margaret's tower

different types of gun (see the illustration on page 26). Sockets surviving in the sides of the gun ports once held timbers for supporting and securing the guns. The upper opening was probably intended for a heavy handgun, the middle one for a larger swivel gun, while the lower rectangular opening probably accommodated a small cannon.

The upper floors contain guardrooms with fireplaces and a latrine which emptied into the moat. Scars in the walls show where the wooden floors used to be. A number of indentations surviving within these scars show that the floor joists were square and crossed the width of the room, supporting thick floorboards running parallel with the joists.

The tower originally had another storey on top, but this was removed at a later date. The large three-light window on the

The interior of the Seymour house

One of the windows in the Seymour house

The kitchen fireplace, inserted in the early seventeenth century, with two ovens in its rear wall

Seymours used much lighter grey limestone, the bedrock immediately below the castle.

The floors of the Seymour house were formed using tall upright joists, not found in the Pomeroy buildings. The upright wooden joists have all since been removed, but they have left sockets in the walls at each of the three upper-floor levels. There are also large square sockets and corbel stones for floor beams which formerly crossed the width of the rooms. These sockets show how the floors were constructed. The joists fitted exactly into the sides of floor beams so that the top and bottom of the floor was flat. Flat undersides of floors were intended for plaster ceilings, so we know that the rooms in the Elizabethan house had plaster ceilings but those in the Pomeroy buildings did not (decorated plaster ceilings were not common in the provinces until around 1560).

The floor levels in the Elizabethan house are often distinct from the surrounding masonry, being marked out by a band of slightly rougher masonry bedded in lesser quality mortar mixed with red earth (sometimes entirely earth). It seems that each time the carpenters laid a floor they, or a gang of roughmasons working alongside them, infilled between the timbers using whatever building materials came most readily to hand. The stone infill was therefore shuttered against the floor frame, and different from the fine coursed masonry above and below which was laid by skilled masons using high-quality white lime mortar.

The ground floor of this range of the courtyard house contained storage rooms and the first floor probably comprised servants' quarters (4). The second floor was taller and had large windows and fireplaces; it was the main floor for the family apartments. The third floor

Detail of one of the ovens in the kitchen fireplace, with a food smoking chamber above

contained additional chambers for family and guests.

A late addition to this range is the ground-floor fireplace with two ovens in the sides for baking. The fireplace was inserted into the building when the eastern storage room was converted into a kitchen, some time in the early seventeenth century. Looking up the flue of this fireplace you can see on the right side a narrow opening which once let smoke from the fire into a small smoking chamber, where food such as bacon, ham and cheese was smoke cured. The two windows in the east wall next to the fireplace were also inserted at this time, one to light the new kitchen, and one to light a room above. *Pass through the buttery and pantry to the main entrance.*

West range: main entrance, screens passage, buttery, pantry and great hall

Stand in the outer courtyard, facing the front wall of the house. The doorway in front of you was the main entrance into the Elizabethan courtyard house (5). Originally the doorway was covered by a three-storey porch, but the porch was taken down when the house was enlarged around 1600. If you look closely you should be able to see two ragged vertical scars in the masonry, one on either side of the doorway, showing where the porch walls once projected into the outer courtyard.

The doorway led into the screens passage, which gave access through the west range to the inner courtyard and had a number of doorways leading off it into the rooms on either side. Leading off its south side are two stone doorways. These led to two service rooms (usually called pantry and buttery) in which food and drink were stored. Above these was a first-floor room which was probably the steward's room, and above that were two floors containing family chambers. On the north side of the screens passage there would have been a fine timber screen with one or more doorways leading into the great hall. Such screens were normally fitted at the lower end of halls to shield the hall from draughts, and to conceal the service doorways into the buttery and pantry. They usually displayed elaborate decoration, especially on the hall side.

The great hall was the tallest room in the courtyard house, and was open from the ground floor to its ceiling at second-floor level. It was a stately room of entrance, as well as a dining hall and common room for the household. The head of the family sometimes laid on great feasts and entertainments here, although the close family usually dined in their more secluded apartments on the second and third floors. The walls would have been covered with panelling and

tapestries. Above the hall were second- and third-floor chambers which formed part of the family and guest apartments.

East range and inner courtyard

The inner courtyard (6) was open to the sky and acted as a light-well, allowing daylight into the many rooms overlooking it. Along the south side of the courtyard was a pentice (covered walkway with a sloping roof) which led from the screens passage of the great hall to the kitchen. The foundations of the pentice were uncovered by excavation in 1991, as were the slate flagstones which once covered the courtyard surface. The wall on the south side of the inner courtyard still retains a projecting slate weathering course which shows where the pentice

Excavation of the inner courtyard in 1991 uncovered slate flagstones dating from about 1600

The remains of a doorway leading from the three-storey gallery into the east range

roof met the wall about 10 ft (3m) above ground level. The pentice sheltered servants delivering food from the kitchen, and had a number of doorways leading off it to various parts of the house. One of these doorways, at the south-west corner of the inner courtyard, opened on to stairs which led to the family apartments on the second and third floors.

The east range was added to the house around 1580-90 to provide more accommodation for a growing household. The family must have been prospering at this time. On the ground floor was a kitchen which replaced an earlier kitchen on the same site. The floors above that contained chambers, possibly for an increased number of servants. The east range was completely refurbished around 1600-10, and provided with more comfortable lodgings on the second and third floors, like those already existing at the same level in the earlier parts of the courtyard house. The present north, south and west walls date from this period, as do all the fireplaces, cupboard recesses and the large windows.

The East Terrace

The east terrace (7) was started around 1600, and was intended to provide a broad promenade for the family to take the air

Excavation of the east terrace in 1991. The terrace was started about 1600 but never completed

and enjoy the views over the wooded valley and fish ponds below. Its construction was abandoned before completion, probably because funding ran out. This was one of three unfinished terraces which would have projected from the north, west and east sides of the house, providing a magnificent setting above the Gatcombe Valley and ponds below (see the illustration on page 5). The engineering for these terraces was formidable: massive retaining walls up to 6ft (nearly 2m) wide and 20ft (6m) high were to be built on to the rock face below the castle to retain the rubble infilling which was to carry level terrace walkways, in places more than 32ft (10m) wide. The east terrace was excavated in 1991 and consolidated by English Heritage.

At the north end of the terrace are the remains of a fifteenth-century angle tower. The tower formed part of the Pomeroy defences and was supported by a large stone buttress extending down the rock face below the castle. It contained a guardroom and had a doorway which opened on to a flight of steps leading down the rock face to a cleft in the rock where spring water was collected. The doorway is protected by another gun port. The east terrace was built around these remains after the tower was no longer needed.

The North Range

About the year 1600 Edward Seymour, Protector Somerset's grandson, launched an ambitious building programme to expand his house into a stately residence. He began on the north side by sweeping away the previous buildings and old Pomeroy defences. These he replaced with a splendid new range built on a much larger scale.

The new north range looked outwards over the Gatcombe Valley, through great towering windows. Some windows were particularly fine constructions, comprising bow windows extending from projecting

The castle as it might have looked in the early seventeenth century, showing the north range and loggia. (Reconstruction by H Gordon Slade, drawn by Terry Ball)

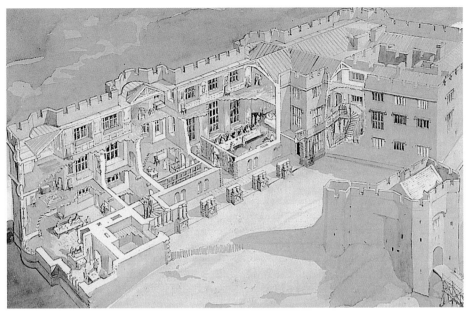

The castle as it might have looked in the early seventeenth century. The drawing has been cut away to reveal the kitchen on the left, the great hall in the centre and the grand staircase on the right. (Reconstruction by H Gordon Slade, drawn by Terry Ball)

square bays. These rose the full height of the building and provided interest and grandeur to the design of the façade, which was symmetrical about its centre in the classical manner. The new north range was the only part of this grand building scheme to be fully completed. It was roofed with slate and fitted with wooden panelling (wainscot), elaborately decorated plaster ceilings and expensive marble fireplaces (known from archaeological and written evidence).

Parlour and great chamber (over)
The parlour (**8**) was a place for informal meals, relaxation, gatherings and games, most often for family use, although in some large houses of the period it was the higher ranking servants, such as the steward, chaplain, secretary and gentlemen of the horse, who ate there. The smaller room immediately to the west of

the parlour formed the entrance to the parlour in the manner of an ante-room, and may have been used for reception or keeping fine tableware and furnishings.

Above these two rooms was the great chamber, the ceremonial centre and finest room of the house. (The great chamber

The remains of the fireplace in the great chamber

together with the great hall are sometimes known as 'state rooms'.) Here the master of the house convened his household and guests for special occasions and formal dinners, often followed by musical entertainment, dances, plays and masques. Occasionally the great chamber was cleared for the 'lying-in-state' of deceased members of the family before funerals. The route to the great chamber from the great hall had to be an impressive stately ascent, so a magnificent staircase was needed.

Site of the great stairs and corridor gallery

Nothing now remains of the great stairs except one or two sockets in the walls where some of the main timbers were anchored (**9**). By 1600 grand staircases were becoming showpieces of elaborate decoration, and wood was often preferred to local stone as it more readily lends itself to detailed carving, and could be painted to simulate exotic stone such as marble.

The stairs were inserted into the northern half of what had previously been the great hall of the Elizabethan courtyard house (a replacement great hall was built in the new north range). Leading off the stairs was a three-storeyed corridor gallery which extended along the north side of the inner courtyard. This provided convenient access to the inner courtyard and to the upper floors of the east range.

Great hall and long gallery (over)

At the centre of the north range was the new great hall (**10**). This rose from ground level through two storeys, and was well lit by a series of tall windows. The windows were so large and so closely spaced that there was more glass than wall, a feature of late Elizabethan and Jacobean 'lantern houses' (a term used to describe these kind of houses, as they shone like lanterns when lit up by candles at night). The immense scale of the windows can be appreciated by

Dining room at Forde House, Newton Abbot, with a fine plaster ceiling, similar to those once at Berry Pomeroy

View across the courtyard towards the north range and the remains of the loggia

looking at the spaces between the surviving tall, thin piers of masonry.

Originally the hall was lined with panelling which has left numerous small holes in the walls where it was hung on wooden fastenings driven into the masonry. Above the panelling was a particularly fine ornamental plaster ceiling. Plaster fragments found at Berry Pomeroy Castle suggest that the ceilings were similar to those at nearby Forde House in Newton Abbot. Plaster finds from archaeological excavations show that there was also at least one elaborate fireplace overmantel, or possibly a decorative frieze, with large supporting caryatids (female figures used as pillars). Glass and lead finds show that the windows were filled with patterned leaded glass.

Above the hall, on the second floor, was a long gallery which stretched the length of the new north range. At more than 207ft (63m) it was among the longest ever built in England, and it was over 26ft (8m) wide. By late Elizabethan and Jacobean times long galleries had become fashionable status symbols, reflecting the rank and social position of their builders who vied among themselves to create larger and better ones. They were usually sparsely furnished, but could be splendidly decorated, approaching the magnificence

of the great chamber. They were often hung with family portraits.

The long gallery at Berry Pomeroy offered wonderful views, stretching over the Devon landscape as far as Dartmoor, and it provided a space for the family and guests to enjoy leisurely promenades, exercise and games. There were wide doorways at either end, so promenaders were able to walk along its entire length without returning the same way.

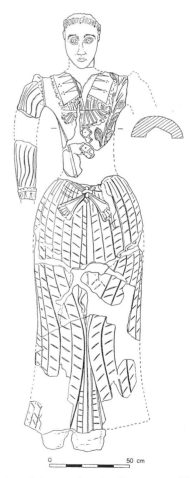

Drawing of the remains of a plaster caryatid which may once have helped support a fireplace overmantel

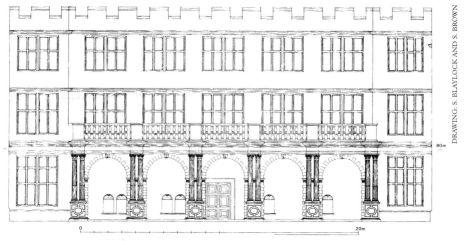

DRAWING: S. BLAYLOCK AND S. BROWN

Reconstruction drawing of the classical-style loggia, based on remains and excavated architectural fragments

Screens passage, loggia and main entrance to the north range

A screens passage (**11**) crossed the lower (west) end of the hall from the main entrance to a doorway (now blocked) which was intended to open on to a terrace overlooking the valley below (this terrace was never built). There would have been a finely carved wooden screen separating the passage from the hall. The main entrance to the screens passage and hall was from the courtyard.

In front of the entrance was a fine loggia (arched walkway built in the classical style). This was a sophisticated display feature of the house, built of limestone imported from Beer in East Devon and crafted by specialist masons. It presented a striking symmetrical façade to what would otherwise have been an asymmetrical ground floor, and linked two stair compartments, one at each end. On its first floor was an open balcony with a balustrade.

After the house was abandoned most of the stone of the loggia was looted by local people who used it for their own buildings, but you can still see the fine Beerstone

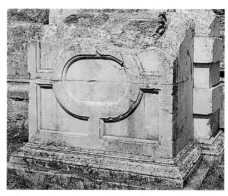

The remains of one of the column pedestals in the loggia

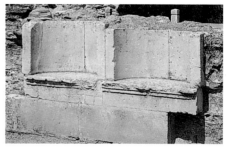

The remains of seats in niches along the back wall of the loggia

View across the loggia to the Seymour house

pedestals for its supporting columns and the bases of seats in niches along its back wall. It has been possible to reconstruct the appearance of the loggia from excavated fragments of carved masonry and a description of the loggia in 1701, when it was already partially in ruins (see the illustration opposite).

To the west of the screens passage was a large, unheated room, which was probably used as a pantry and buttery. Beneath this is a cellar cut from the limestone which was kept damp and cool by having rainwater fed into it through a culvert. The water would have covered the rock to a depth of around 1 ft (30cm), and gradually drained away, to be replenished at the next rainfall. The cellar must have had a raised wooden floor above water level. It seems likely to have served as a beer cellar.

Kitchen block and lodgings

At the west end of the north range were the new kitchen services (12). Two large fireplaces survive in the main kitchen. The fireplace to the west has a recess on each side, one for a boiler, and the other possibly

for a kitchen boy to sit and turn the roasting spit. Another fireplace with two ovens set into its back, evidently for baking, survives in a separate room (probably the bakery or pantry) which lay to the south of the main kitchen. This fireplace is the only one in the north range to retain remnants of fine decorative stone mouldings, which in this case are carved from red sandstone from the Torbay area. A small inner room was probably for stores or may have been used by kitchen officials. To the east of the kitchen was a servery where food was dished for the table and collected by serving staff. Below this was another cellar which may well have been used for washing pans and dishes, as it had its own water supply and was accessible from the kitchen by a flight of steps.

The first floor at this end of the range was occupied by a suite of fine lodgings containing four spacious rooms. Another large chamber on the second floor, which opened onto the long gallery, probably formed part of the same suite. Excavated finds of finely decorated plasterwork prove that at least some of these rooms had plaster ceilings and fireplace overmantels as ornate as those in the 'state' rooms at the other end of the north range, so they were clearly meant to offer high quality accommodation for either family or guests.

The building work left incomplete

The cost of the new building work appears to have exceeded the limits of the family's financial resources as the grand scheme was suddenly halted, never to be brought to completion. The broad terraces which were intended to surround the house were barely begun before they were abandoned. This meant that the kitchen and beer cellar in the north range were never provided with external entrances, so that supplies must have been unloaded and carried to them through the loggia, a most unsatisfactory arrangement. Even comparatively simple

tasks such as clearing unwanted outcrops of
bedrock from in front of the loggia were left
undone. It appears, therefore, that the
north range, despite being fitted and
decorated throughout the interior, stood
among unfinished building works, and it is
questionable whether all parts of it ever
functioned fully as intended. Indeed, an
inventory made of the house in the later
seventeenth century suggests that the whole
western end of the north range was later
adapted for more humble, ancillary uses,
such as brewing and cider-making, perhaps
with stores or servants' quarters above.

Courtyard

*Returning to the main courtyard, you will see
limestone bedrock protruding through the
present lawn in places.* This interrupts the
view of the loggia, and impedes progress
around the courtyard (**13**). It would
certainly have been cleared away had the
grand building scheme been completed.

*Toothing-stones project from the kitchen block,
showing that a west range was intended but
never built*

Uncleared bedrock in front of the loggia, showing that the building work was never completed

Looking up at the kitchen block to the north-west, there is good evidence to show that a west range of buildings was intended. Projecting toothing-stones have been left exposed on the south side, where the walls of the intended buildings were to join. From the courtyard it is also possible to see how the new north range broke through the line of the old Pomeroy curtain wall. There can be little doubt that the rest of the old Pomeroy defences, including the gatehouse, would have been torn down and replaced by new buildings had the proposed scheme gone ahead.

Historic Surroundings

Deer park, fish ponds, lime kilns and quarries

Several quarries for building stone can be found near the castle, the largest being the slate quarry now occupied by the car park. Other quarries in the area were for limestone which provided lime for building and, from at least the eighteenth century, for liming farmers' fields. Lime kilns are numerous in the area. The nearest one stands beside the road in the Gatcombe Valley. *Those who wish to enjoy*

Aerial view of the castle, looking north

SKYSCAN

the attractive scenery of the wooded Gatcombe Valley should walk through the car park and follow the path down through the woods. The enclosing wall of the deer park, owned by the Pomeroys since at least the thirteenth century, can be seen descending into the Gatcombe Valley where it crosses the brook by a small, specially built bridge. The wall can still be seen in many places. Remarkably it still stands in places more than 10ft (3m) high, although parts of it have been rebuilt in more recent times. From here it is a short and level walk to the open part of the valley from where there is a good view of the castle.

The Gatcombe Brook was at one time dammed to form a series of three fish ponds. The earth dams are still just visible where they cross the valley. The ponds are not closely datable, but belong to the medieval or early post-medieval period. Fish ponds provided food for the table in winter, and were highly prized assets of landowners of manorial and noble status. From the eighteenth to the twentieth century the top pond was used as a reservoir for water which was directed along a leat to power Castle Mill and a

The deer park wall is carried across the Gatcombe Brook by a small bridge

nineteenth-century saw mill further down the valley.

View of the medieval deer park wall surrounding the castle, with Dartmoor in the distance

History

The Pomeroys

The Pomeroy family originally came from a French village called La Pommeraye near Falaise in Normandy. Ralf de Pomeroy fought at the time of the Norman Conquest, and may have taken part in the siege of Exeter in 1068. He was rewarded by William the Conqueror with fifty-seven manors in Devon, including Berry Pomeroy, his most valuable property, and two more in Somerset. His estate was the fifth largest baronial landholding in Devon. Before the Conquest, the land at Berry was owned by a Saxon called Alric.

In the following centuries the Pomeroys frequently held high office in Devon, including the position of sheriff, but took little part in the affairs of state and country. They experienced mixed fortunes and sometimes leased or sold their properties to others. In the thirteenth and fourteenth centuries, they consolidated their landholding in south Devon. By 1268 they had founded a borough called Bridgetown on their land bordering the River Dart, opposite Totnes. The borough brought in rents from tenants and provided a good regular income. The first reference to a deer park at Berry Pomeroy occurs in 1207, when Henry Pomeroy paid 10 marks (a mark was originally the value of one mark weight of pure silver, and not a coin) to enclose it. In 1305, the park is described as containing 100 acres of pasture with deer.

The Pomeroys had a number of homes, including one at Tregony in Cornwall, and a manor house at Berry Pomeroy which is described as a 'hall with chambers' in a survey of 1293. The manor house stood in the village of Berry Pomeroy on the site of the present manor house, next to the church, and not within the deer park like the later castle. Family records frequently mention the house but no castle at Berry Pomeroy up to the mid-fifteenth century. In 1428 Edward Pomeroy and his family were attacked and violently removed from the house by a rival family faction. A document of 1496 mentions two residences belonging to the Pomeroys in their manor of Berry Pomeroy, the castle and a separate manor house, almost certainly the one they had occupied since at least the late thirteenth century.

The last Pomeroy owner of the manor and castle was Thomas Pomeroy, who appears to have fallen into deep financial problems and was forced to sell the castle, the manor and other nearby properties. In 1547, after a series of complicated exchanges involving a third party, Sir Wemond Carew, the castle and surrounding properties were sold to Edward Seymour, the first Duke of Somerset, who became known as Protector Somerset.

The Seymours

Edward Seymour claimed descent from Wido St Maur, who took his name from St Maur-sur-Loire in Touraine, and who fought with William the Conqueror at the Battle of Hastings (Seymour is an anglicisation of St Maur). In the thirteenth century the family held Penhow Castle and other properties in Monmouthshire. By the fifteenth century Edward's ancestors had moved to Wiltshire and settled into gentry life. The family rose to national prominence when Jane Seymour, Edward's sister, married Henry VIII in 1536. Jane died aged

Portrait thought to be of Edward Seymour,
first Duke of Somerset, by an unknown artist

twenty-eight, having given birth to Prince Edward, who was to become Edward VI upon Henry's death in 1547. At the time, Edward VI was but a boy, and Edward Seymour, his uncle, was appointed the King's guardian until he came of age.

Edward Seymour was an ambitious and daring soldier who rose to become the most powerful man in England. His military successes in both Scotland and France, and his close relationship with the centre of power, first Cardinal Wolsey, then Henry VIII and finally Edward VI, brought many titles and offices, including Viscount Beauchamp (1536), Earl of Hertford (1537), and first Duke of Somerset (1547). During the first two years of Edward's reign, he acted as High Steward of England, Treasurer of the Exchequer, and Earl Marshal and Protector of the Realm. He acquired vast wealth and property, and actively pursued an interest in architecture, becoming one of the most innovative patrons of building

in the new classical style from France and Italy. But he also acquired political enemies who overthrew him as Protector in 1549 and eventually saw him beheaded in 1552. Most of his extensive properties, acquired while he held power, were taken into the hands of the Crown.

Protector Somerset had married twice. By an act of Parliament passed in 1540, he made it clear that he wished the family honours and estates to pass to the male line of his second marriage or, failing that, to his male descendants by his first wife. In 1553 his eldest surviving son by his first marriage, Sir Edward Seymour, acquired Berry Pomeroy, and soon after made it his home. The fall of his father compounded the problems of his inheritance, but with

Portrait of Jane Seymour, after Holbein, from
Woburn Abbey

help from Sir John Thynne, the builder of Longleat House (who had been the Protector's steward and supervisor of building works), he made a bargain with the King and Sir John which granted him the castle and (by 1558) the surrounding manor. He married in 1562 and settled into family life and administering his estates. He became a respected county gentleman, and was made Sheriff of Devon in 1583. In 1588, when the threat of invasion from Spain loomed ever greater, he was appointed by Queen Elizabeth to raise troops to defend the Devon shores. He died in 1593, leaving his eldest son, another Edward, in a far better position to restore the family's former high regard and honour. He had established a new family seat at Berry Pomeroy, and built a house within the old castle defences with few, if any, rivals in Devon.

This next Edward, the grandson of the Protector, was ably suited to carry his father's ambitions further. He had already been Sheriff of Devon (c.1583) and was made Vice-Admiral of Cornwall in 1586. He was MP for Devon from 1590 until 1611, and again Sheriff in 1595 and 1605. He procured the title of baronet in 1611 from James I, and entered into a beneficial marriage with Elizabeth, daughter of Sir Arthur Champernowne from nearby Dartington Hall. It was in his time that the grand scheme to enlarge the house was started. A local historian called Risdon, who was writing within living memory of this period, tells us that it was this Sir Edward, the first baronet, who made the building into 'a very stately house'.

The Seymour family continued to reside at Berry Pomeroy until some time between 1688, when an inventory of the rooms was made, and 1701, when John Prince described the building as already in ruins. They had remained county gentry, and moved from their unfinished grand house to a more up-to-date country house which they had built on another of their properties at Maiden Bradley in Wiltshire. In due course, the dukedom passed to their branch of the family when the junior male line failed in 1750. Consequently, the house at Berry Pomeroy was never occupied by dukes, although its ruins are owned by the current Duke of Somerset.

Architecture

The Pomeroy castle defences

The Pomeroy defences were well organised in a military fashion, and included provision for a small garrison employed by the family. There were guardrooms in each of the towers from which sentries could patrol the wall walks, passages and battlements. Each guardroom controlled a length of the curtain wall (the south curtain was divided into two, and patrolled from the east tower of the gatehouse and from St Margaret's tower). Each section of the wall was separated from the next, so that if the

View through the gate, showing the vertical groove which once held a portcullis

defences were breached at one point the defenders could rally at another and prevent the castle from being entirely overrun.

The tower basements could be manned quickly and were designed specifically for defence by hand guns and small cannon. The three gun ports in the basement of St Margaret's tower show a sophisticated developed form with three superimposed openings capable of sustaining near-continuous fire from three different weapons. While one was being reloaded another could be deployed. The design is unique in this country, but a few similar examples dating from around 1450 are known from Germany. One important difference, however, is the double splay in the lower rectangular opening intended for a

Stairs leading up from the gatehouse basement

View through the triple gun part in the basement of St Margaret's tower, showing openings for three types of gun, including a small cannon at the bottom

small cannon mounted on a stock (hollowed out piece of wood). This allowed greater traverse of the gun, and its introduction marks an important stage in the evolution of gun ports, from the medieval form to those of the early modern era which were built with a pronounced external splay.

The Pomeroys appear to have taken advice from a military engineer from the Continent, where artillery design was more advanced. The more frequently occurring form of gun port used at Berry Pomeroy, a simple slit with circular opening at its centre or base, is of a more common type, and was often used elsewhere in this period, sometimes in conjunction with straight-sided gun ports for large cannon, as at the nearby artillery castle begun at Dartmouth in 1481.

The gatehouse has a fairly close parallel, albeit a distant one, in the

Raglan Castle, Monmouthshire, remodelled after 1461, has similar gatehouse towers to those at Berry Pomeroy, as well as numerous gun ports

gatehouse built at Raglan Castle (Wales) in the mid- or late fifteenth century. This also has twinned, forward-pointing or 'beaked' towers with gun ports at basement level, and contains other features thought to have been influenced by French military architecture. The portcullis and machicolation at Berry Pomeroy recall similar defensive features added to the previously undefended Compton Castle near Torquay in the late fifteenth or early sixteenth century.

The Elizabethan courtyard house

The tall compact house built by the Seymours around a small inner courtyard around 1560 had an unostentatious but effective façade, with an emphasis on uniformity and symmetry. The relatively symmetrical design was complete save only for the intentional omission of ground-floor windows in front of the hall, which was thus marked out. There are no

comparable houses of this date known in Devon, so it seems that the Seymours found inspiration elsewhere. This type of house became fashionable among the gentry of the Midlands and the north of England in the late sixteenth and early seventeenth century, as at Thorp Salvin near Sheffield (c.1570s), Barlborough Hall in Derbyshire (1580s, probably designed by the master mason Robert Smythson), and Gawthorpe near Burnley (1600-5). A similar house of pioneering design was built in the 1550s by the courtier Sir Nicholas Poyntz (a member of Protector Somerset's circle) as a hunting lodge at Newark Park, near Ozleworth in Gloucestershire.

North range

The north range was built around 1600 as the first stage in an adventurous scheme of enlargement which was never completed. The Seymour family clearly intended to erect themselves a residence to compare with the great country houses which had sprung up throughout many parts of England during the stable and prosperous years of Queen Elizabeth's reign. At the highest social levels, those with close connections with the crown built on an extraordinarily sumptuous scale, fitting for the reception of the Queen herself, together with her entire retinue, should she decide to visit when she travelled the counties each summer. These visits were known as the Royal Progresses. Previous monarchs had undertaken similar Progresses, visiting crown estates, great magnates and monasteries, but Elizabeth cultivated competition among her most ambitious courtiers, and expected lavish entertainment. The builders vied with each other to gain the Queen's admiration and approval, and often exceeded the limits of their resources. Moreover, others aspired to emulate this spirit. Those who held high office in the counties, together with a few private gentlemen of sufficient means, embarked on building projects of almost equal magnificence.

The impressive scale of the new building work at Berry Pomeroy must have sent out signals reflecting the family's social ambitions, even though the likelihood of a royal visit was remote (neither Elizabeth nor her successor, James I, ever did travel as far west as Devon). The family may possibly have been spurred into building by the visit paid by Queen Elizabeth to Sir Edward Seymour's half brother, the Earl of Hertford, who in 1591 was obliged to erect numerous temporary timber buildings at his country home at Elvetham, Hampshire, in order to accommodate the Queen and her court. The Seymours' house at Berry Pomeroy cannot be counted among the very few exceptionally grand houses of the period which were provided with two principal suites of accommodation, one for the owner's household and another specifically intended for royal visits, such as Holdenby House, Audley End and Hatfield House. However, it still contained numerous high quality lodgings capable of accommodating both family and important guests. Had the building work not halted after the completion of the north range, it seems likely that even more lodgings would have been provided within a range on the west of the entrance court.

Precisely which of the lodgings were intended for the family and which for guests we cannot know for certain. By comparison with similar houses elsewhere, we might expect the principal family

The east front of Audley End in Essex, begun in 1603. The large bay windows, dating from the eighteenth and nineteenth centuries, are similar to those once at Berry Pomeroy

The architecture of Longleat House, Wiltshire, completed around 1580, probably inspired the Seymours

lodgings to be sited above the kitchen, like those at the west end of the new north range, and for the 'best lodgings', suitable for guests, to lie at the opposite end, leading off the best staircase and placed close to the great chamber or withdrawing chamber. Whatever arrangements were intended at the outset, these probably had to be modified after the building programme was curtailed midway, an event which must have represented a disappointing blow to the family's aspirations. The abandonment of the terraces and the unsightly bedrock protruding directly in front of the loggia tell their own story. If the family's hopes of grand entertainment had to be scaled down as seems likely, then how was the surfeit of lodgings used? It is possible that sometimes the house accommodated more than one generation of the family, each forming a semi-independent household. Indeed, a quotation relating to the birth of Sir Edward Seymour, the third Baronet, in about the year 1610 describes the castle mansion as then undergoing a 'rebuilding', and that his mother did not like the 'music of axes and hammers', so temporarily removed herself to the lowly vicarage nearby, where he was born. And since we know that the child's grandfather was still alive at this time, it seems reasonable to assume that the house was occupied by both an elder and younger generation.

The scale and design of the north range has no comparison within Devon, and must have been influenced by great Elizabethan country houses elsewhere in England, such as Longleat House in Wiltshire. Indeed, the Seymour family had close connections with the builder of Longleat, Sir John Thynne (who had been Protector Somerset's steward), as well as the Queen's ministers, Lord Burleigh and his son Sir Robert Cecil, who were among the greatest builders of their time.

The Elizabethan age was an exciting experimental period of architectural development, which combined elements from traditional English building with new ideas concerning design from the Continent, such as classical symmetry, proportion and detail from France and Italy, as well as more vigorous, ornate decorative motifs from the Low Countries, often in the form of strapwork (as if cut from leather or parchment). Each of these major building projects was a personal enterprise of the owner, and took on a distinctly individual nature, producing variations in design which have led modern writers to describe them as 'prodigy houses', or brilliant individual creations.

The north range at Berry Pomeroy follows a traditional English layout with rooms of differing sizes (on the ground floor: great hall, screens passage, parlour and service rooms). The varying proportions of the rooms was masked by a regular, symmetrical exterior influenced by the new classical style. And yet the design of the exterior made great display of towering bay and bow windows, features peculiar to English architecture and not found on the Continent.

Large bow windows featured in the design of other late sixteenth- and early seventeenth-century English country houses, such as Kirby Hall in Northamptonshire (where a double bow-fronted wing was added towards the end of the sixteenth century), Burton Agnes Hall in Humberside (c.1601), Audley End in Essex (begun in 1603), Wootton Lodge in Staffordshire (c.1608-11) and Lilford Hall in Northamptonshire (1635).

Two of the bow windows at Berry Pomeroy projected from square window-bays, a distinctive arrangement also found in the front of the Manor House at Bradford-on-Avon (1590s). Some buildings of the period, including the north range at Berry Pomeroy, had so many windows that the term 'lantern house' was sometimes used to describe them, as they shone like lanterns when lit up by candles at night.

The loggia was one of the showpieces of the house, built in a pure classical style by specialist masons. It was inspired by designs published in book form by Sebastiano Serlio, an Italian architect who moved to the French court where he completed a great treatise on classical architecture before his death in 1554. Various versions of his book and its illustrations circulated widely throughout western Europe in the second half of the sixteenth century. It had a considerable influence on Elizabethan builders in England, although the text was not printed in an English translation until 1611.

Despite the classical form of the loggia, the surviving pedestals which once supported its columns are decorated with strapwork in the north-European style. It is interesting that the motif, an oval with vertical and horizontal arms, has an exact parallel in the loggia at Longford Castle,

Longford Castle, Wiltshire, built around 1580, has oval motifs on either side of the loggia which are almost identical to those at Berry Pomeroy

Wiltshire (c.1580-91), although similar examples can be found closer by on a number of church monuments of the time, including the Seymour monument of 1613 in Berry Pomeroy church.

The loggia also retains remnants of seats set in alcoves in its rear wall. According to a description written in 1701 by the antiquary John Prince, rector of Berry Pomeroy church, these alcoves were capped with a scallop-shell motif. Similar shell-headed alcoves are found in association with loggias at a number of other houses in the West Country, for instance at Longford and Old Wardour Castles, both in Wiltshire (the latter remodelled 1576-8), and Cranborne Manor, Dorset (remodelled 1608-11). Two more survive beside one of the entrance doorways at Lulworth Castle, Dorset (c.1588-1607).

The impressive long gallery provided another high-status flourish which reflected the family's social ambitions. Such galleries were initially inspired by French examples, but in the second half of the sixteenth century English builders began to develop them into grand rooms of extraordinary length for indoor recreation and exercise, quite possibly prompted by the often inclement English weather. Long galleries commonly became part of the state suite of apartments in great Elizabethan and Jacobean country houses, and were incorporated into the buildings with an originality and ingenuity seldom matched abroad. For comparison with the gallery at Berry Pomeroy (207ft/63m long), other notable examples were built at Worksop Manor, Nottinghamshire (212ft/64m; a remodelled hunting lodge completed 1586); Slaugham Place, Sussex, (212ft/64m; 1570s-1580s); Audley End, Essex (190ft/58m; begun in 1603); Hampton Court, the Queen's Long Gallery (180ft/55m; 1536-7); Montacute

House, Somerset (170ft/52m; 1590s); Parham, Sussex (166ft/51m; 1570s-1580s); and Hardwick New Hall, Derbyshire (160ft/49m; 1590-3).

All the late Elizabethan and Jacobean houses mentioned above display some similarity with the north range at Berry Pomeroy, so it is clear that the Seymour family were keen to keep up with contemporary architectural developments from around the country, incorporating design ideas from various sources and, in their turn, influencing others. Like the builders of many great houses of the period, they probably sought advice, and perhaps designs, from skilled craftsmen and master masons recommended by their friends and associates (there was no equivalent of the architectural profession of our day).

There is no written record to tell us any names, but the above list of comparable buildings suggests a possible connection with two particular master masons, Robert Smythson and William Arnold. Robert Smythson drew plans for Burton Agnes Hall, worked on the remodelling of Old Wardour Castle, was probably closely associated with the design of Wootton Lodge and Barlborough Hall, and possibly The Hall, Bradford-on-Avon. William Arnold worked at Cranborne Manor, The Hall, Bradford-on-Avon, and probably Lulworth Castle. Robert Smythson is not known to have travelled to this part of the country, but could have sent drawings for the design.

William Arnold was the leading member of a West Country family of masons, and the most likely of all the known master masons working at the time to have influenced the design of the loggia. He may even have travelled to the site to advise on or organise the work, as he did for the construction of Wadham College in Oxford in 1610, a job which he undertook with twenty-nine men who travelled with him from Somerset. The Seymours' connection with Sir Robert Cecil may well have been significant in developing contacts. He knew of and admired Smythson's work, and employed Arnold at Cranborne Manor.

The new north range looked outwards, like other grand late Elizabethan and Jacobean houses, rather than inwards, as the earlier courtyard house had done. The unfinished terraces which were intended to grace three sides of the house may have been inspired by the Great Terrace at Windsor Castle, constructed in 1571-8, or by the many hanging terraces built in Italy and France.

The cost of building the Elizabethan courtyard house with its north range addition was said to have been in excess of £20,000, a vast sum in those days. The expenditure appears to have caused the family serious hardship. In June 1611 Edward Seymour wrote to his son Walter, who was studying at Oxford, urging economy as his debts were crushing.

The building works were halted abruptly, never to be completed.

A Romantic Ruin

After the castle was abandoned around 1700 it was stripped of valuable materials such as lead from the roofs and reusable timber beams, and left to fall into decay. In the eighteenth century the ruins became overgrown with ivy and were the haunt of nesting jackdaws. Artists came to make romantic drawings and paintings, and antiquarians mused over its past. Legends and mysterious stories of hauntings soon began to multiply among the local population. In the nineteenth century, holidaymakers from the seaside resort of Torbay made the short journey to take a pleasant stroll around the castle's remains. The ruins were kept up by the Duke of Somerset's estate workers, who patched and consolidated the crumbling walls, and inserted new timbers to replace missing ones.

SPINK AND SON

A romantic view of the castle from the Gatcombe Valley, painted in the late eighteenth or early nineteenth century by Thomas Rowlandson

Ghostly Tales

Berry Pomeroy is reputed to be one of the most haunted castles in Britain. A number of people claim to have seen ghosts in and around the castle, and many more have had strange experiences there. The basement of St Margaret's tower is allegedly haunted by the 'White Lady', the ghost of Lady Margaret Pomeroy who, according to legend, was imprisoned here by her jealous sister, Lady Eleanor. Several people claim to have seen her or felt her presence in the tower. The castle is also thought to be haunted by a figure known as the 'Blue Lady'. A member of the Pomeroy family, she allegedly had a child by her own father and later strangled it. Some claim to have seen her beckoning to them in the castle grounds, while others have heard a baby's cries. Many have reported feeling suddenly very cold in the castle, and some have heard strange sounds such as doors slamming, although there are no longer any doors in the castle. Several people have had problems with cameras at Berry Pomeroy: figures have appeared on photographs who did not seem to be there at the time; whole rolls of film, or just specific shots of the castle, have come out blank; and even an ITV camera crew could not get their equipment to work when they came down one night to take some pictures of the castle. The surrounding area also seems to be prone to ghostly sightings. The figure of a woman in old-fashioned dress has been seen on a nearby wooden footbridge, while a cavalier has also been reported walking a few inches above the road. Some people even seem to have slipped back in time near the castle. Two women were driving down a lane leading to the mill, when they sensed a strange atmosphere. As they approached the ramshackle old mill, they noticed a young girl sitting on the wall outside, wearing a dirty, sack-like dress. They were quite frightened and turned the car round and drove off. A couple of weeks later, one of the women went back and the mill looked completely different. The roof had been re-thatched and a whole new wing had been added. Similarly, a family took a helicopter trip over the castle and claimed that they had seen it with turrets and roofs, and smoke coming out of the chimneys.

Piecing Together the Evidence

Much fresh evidence has come to light to help our understanding of the castle buildings. Finds from excavations between 1980 and 1995 have been particularly useful in the dating of successive phases of building. For instance, a group of finds belonging to the years around 1600 were found among the construction levels of the north range, including fragments of imported Chinese porcelain (Wan Li, Ming dynasty), and very early clay pipes for smoking tobacco. Another method for dating buildings is by dendrochronology (tree-ring dating) which provides a felling date for timbers preserved in the structure. In the case of the north range, an oak lintel which was built into its west end was shown to have been felled between the years 1591 and 1601.

PHOTO: S.BROWN

Excavated finds of Chinese porcelain and other imported pottery, together with early clay tobacco pipes, help date the construction of the north range to about 1600. A modern coin shows the scale.

By plotting structural differences in the surviving remains (both above and below ground), and finding inserted (or blocked) features such as windows and doorways, it

Plaster fragment of a horse's head from one of the ceilings

has been possible to build up a picture of how the castle changed over time. A study of the architectural styles and details used in the buildings has also been important for dating the various stages of its development. Written and pictorial records are helpful, as they describe or show the buildings at particular dates. Building historians and archaeologists have pieced together all these various strands of evidence, so that it is now possible to appreciate the castle's place in history more clearly.

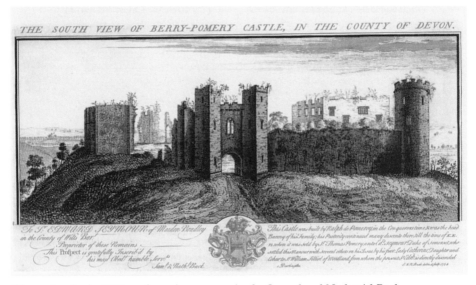

THE SOUTH VIEW OF BERRY-POMERY CASTLE, IN THE COUNTY OF DEVON.

The castle ruins in 1734, as shown in an engraving by Samuel and Nathaniel Buck

Conservation

Management by English Heritage has meant the consolidation of the ruins, the laying out of the site to allow better access for visitors (and to deny trespass) and the re-roofing of the gatehouse chamber to protect the fine wall-painting in its oratory. Works followed detailed examination of the site both by excavation and structural analysis. These investigations meant that repair proposals could be developed from a position of greater knowledge and deeper understanding of the site and its development and of the techniques used in its construction. Where possible, in recent works, matching materials and techniques have been used. This has involved slaking lime on site and adopting a 'soft' approach to finishes.

In some places intervention has been dramatic (if inconspicuous), such as the restraint in the kitchen block. In other places it has been designed to assist interpretation, such as the beam stubs supporting masonry over historic beam sockets. In yet other places it is relatively conspicuous where concealed repairs would have led to greater loss of the original fabric, but such props are easily

Props inserted into the fabric of the building to prevent it from collapsing

reversible. Improvements, such as lime-washing of the gatehouse passages, are effective but also reversible.

The philosophy of recent repairs has been minimal intervention, matching existing materials, the use of traditional materials and techniques, protection before display and reversibility. Visitor access and safety have been prime considerations and, related to intervention, have been designed to be inconspicuous and harmonious.

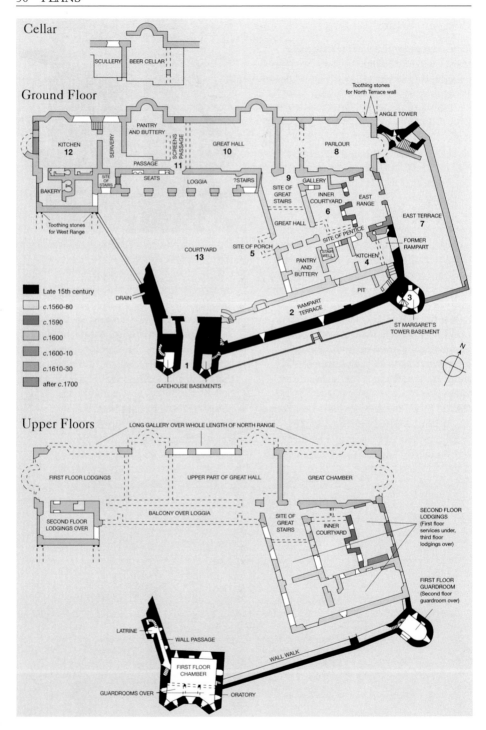

Cellar

SCULLERY | BEER CELLAR

Ground Floor

Toothing stones for North Terrace wall

ANGLE TOWER

KITCHEN 12

SERVERY

PANTRY AND BUTTERY

SCREENS PASSAGE

GREAT HALL 10

PARLOUR 8

PASSAGE

11

9

GALLERY

BAKERY

SITE OF STAIRS

SEATS

LOGGIA

?STAIRS

SITE OF GREAT STAIRS

INNER COURTYARD

EAST RANGE

EAST TERRACE 7

6

Toothing stones for West Range

GREAT HALL

SITE OF PENTICE

FORMER RAMPART

COURTYARD 13

SITE OF PORCH 5

PANTRY AND BUTTERY

STAIR WELL

KITCHEN 4

DRAIN

Late 15th century

c.1560-80

c.1590

c.1600

c.1600-10

c.1610-30

after c.1700

PIT

RAMPART TERRACE

2

3

ST MARGARET'S TOWER BASEMENT

1

GATEHOUSE BASEMENTS

N

Upper Floors

LONG GALLERY OVER WHOLE LENGTH OF NORTH RANGE

FIRST FLOOR LODGINGS

UPPER PART OF GREAT HALL

GREAT CHAMBER

SECOND FLOOR LODGINGS OVER

BALCONY OVER LOGGIA

SITE OF GREAT STAIRS

INNER COURTYARD

SECOND FLOOR LODGINGS (First floor services under, third floor lodgings over)

FIRST FLOOR GUARDROOM (Second floor guardroom over)

LATRINE

WALL PASSAGE

WALL WALK

FIRST FLOOR CHAMBER

GUARDROOMS OVER

ORATORY